The Myth, a Secret and an Obsession
Harming Women and Men

By
George Franklin Rosselot

The Myth, a Secret and an Obsession
Copyright ©2006 by George Franklin Rosselot
Tallahassee, Florida ~ All rights reserved.

ISBN #0-9779579-0-X

Printed in the United States of America. All rights reserved under International Copyright Law. Contents and/or cover may not be reproduced in whole or in part in any form without the express written consent of the author and publisher.

Cover Design by Mim Davis

Irving, Texas 75062

The research of the National Institute for Mental Health (N.I.M.H.) states that one out of four women have been sexually traumatized. I have found over these past thirty years of clinical practice as a psychotherapist that eight out of ten women that I worked with were abused before eighteen years of age.

**"Over 95% of the women I have counseled were liberated and healed of hurts and the related consequences by simply hearing and understanding these basic principals and knowing about
The Myth."**

George Franklin Rosselot

TABLE OF CONTENTS

FOREWARD	7
INTRODUCTION	11
DEDICATIONS	15
ACKNOWLEDGMENTS OF APPRECIATION	17

CHAPTER I

The Myth	23
WOMEN'S TRAUMAS	*23*
THE SECRET	*24*

CHAPTER II

Discovering the Secret	31
GUILT AND PUNISHMENT	*31*
THREE QUESTIONS	*32*
ADDITIONAL TRAUMA INDICATORS	*36*

CHAPTER III

Illustrations of Levels of Trauma	39
LEVEL ONE	*40*
LEVEL TWO	*43*
LEVEL THREE	*45*

CHAPTER IV

The Result	53
OPPRESSION	*53*
GRIEF	*54*

CHAPTER V

The Obsession   59
MEN'S TRAUMAS   59
THE ANTIDOTE   64

CHAPTER VI

The Recovery   67
HEALING APPROACHES   67

CHAPTER VII

The New Vision
LOVE   77
FRIENDSHIP   81

CHAPTER VIII

The Conclusion   87

APPENDIX I

Supplemental Reading   89

APPENDIX II

Resources   91

APPENDIX III

About the Author   93

FOREWARD

I have known George Rosselot for many years. At one point, I was in private practice with him at Eastwood Counseling Clinic here in Tallahassee, Florida. He established the clinic as a multidisciplinary practice of psychologists, psychiatrists, clinical social workers, marriage and family therapists, mental health counselors and counseling psychologists to meet the needs of individuals seeking therapy.

Mr. Rosselot has pioneered in many areas contributing to the health and well being of individuals seeking therapy. A few highlights of his accomplishments and special areas of expertise are his unique, practical, and therapeutic approaches relating to women's issues, concepts of marriage as a friendship, family roles and relationships as well as revolutionary concepts relating to the academic classroom and its role in modeling our youth and society as a whole.

He has also contributed to professional organizations as being President of the Florida Association of Marriage and Family Therapy (FAMFT), serving on committees for the American Association of Marriage and Family Therapy (AAMFT), and working extensively with the Florida Legislature to acquire laws for therapists

FORWARD

in order to provide confidentiality and privileged communication for clients and their therapists.

Mr. Rosselot was honored as a Fellow by AAMFT for his legislative accomplishments establishing Marriage and Family Therapy as a profession by State Law. He received recognition for outstanding leadership at the AAMFT National Convention in 1986; was issued the first Marriage and Family Therapy license by the Florida Department of Professional Regulation (DPR) honoring his accomplishments with regard to the first licensing of Marriage and Family Therapists in the State. In addition, DPR, AAMFT administrators and various division leaders have called him on as a consultant over the years.

As a clinician in full time private practice, he has dealt with the complex issues where law, regulation, and intra-professional systems mesh at a grassroots level. He was one of the leaders and communicators to activate and design a Coalition of Interdisciplinary Professionals within the State of Florida. He has extensive understanding and experience in the political arena involving legislative and professional issues.

As a professional, I have known Mr. Rosselot to be constantly searching to contribute to others for their best interest and the best interest of society. He is a pioneer in his field and is now making a contribution to a larger audience through publishing what he has found to be helpful in providing new knowledge and insights

FORWARD

for individuals to be able to live creative, productive and fulfilling lives.

I am fully aware of his concepts and am confident in their results. I feel they will make a difference and lead individuals to discover the true richness of everyday life.

Donald R. Bardill, Ph.D., LPSY
Professor Emeritus, Florida State University
Past National President,
American Association of Marriage and Family Therapists

INTRODUCTION

This book provides the dynamics as to why sexually traumatized women are highly attracted and can become addicted to men who abuse them verbally and/or physically. The society teachings and physical factors "set the woman up." When a woman learns the correct information she is set free and can heal. She no longer has the attraction to men who will harm her and has a renewed sense of living.

In my experience, the majority of cases with sexual issues were not the initial reason for women entering therapy. My greatest discovery was in finding out how a girl or woman answers three questions I have developed. Her response determines if she had been sexually invaded and the degree of invasion and trauma. Once discovered, I was able to apply specific methods of treatment through therapy. It has proven to be very effective in a patient's recovery. The discovery of this method to uncover these traumas and the healing resolutions are shared in this book.

INTRODUCTION

There are two mistaken beliefs revealed and two new insights presented relating to society's sexual beliefs between and about men and women. One of the mistaken beliefs is that women are responsible for men's sexual response and attitude. Women who are sexually invaded, from mild situations to major abusive events, hold a secret that reinforces them to believe they are responsible for a man's sexual response. When this mistaken belief and secret are revealed, healing can begin to take place.

These new understandings can make a major difference in the choices a woman makes in a male friendship or lifetime mate. Connecting the "myth" and "secret" enhances the lives of women and men and creates a lasting and creative relationship. The revelation of this truth produces a healthy friendship that is freed from the societal mistaken beliefs and "trap!"

As simple as it seems, I have seen this concept completely liberate women. They no longer punish themselves. They cease to pick men that hurt them, they start loving themselves and feeling good about who they are. Women have new insights and realize their attractions are due to prior traumas – this "knowing" or "ah-ha" experience corrects their internal beliefs. It provides

INTRODUCTION

freedom from their emotional bondage and truly creates a new way and a new life – a new walk in life. The woman is not to blame. <u>*Even more so, the healing is permanent*</u>. It provides healing for the rest of their lives.   They are no longer trapped by the myth and the secret ... they are now free to explore and enjoy their lives in every aspect with unlimited potential.

It is my hope that by helping individuals heal, by learning this new knowledge, it will be a step to overcoming the pain in our society. My purpose in writing this book is to be able to help people stop hurting and start rebuilding their lives because they have learned about the myth and the secret, and through this understanding have a fresh insight. These concepts, which seem simple in explanation, yet are complex in their totality, will help individuals to be free, to move forward and to explore a wonderful, beautiful life for themselves.

In his many years of experience as a psychotherapist, George Rosselot has collected overwhelming evidence to support his contentions about what isn't working in contemporary marital and family life. In an effort to help his clients, he has carefully constructed a working model of marriage that evolves beyond the traditional model based primarily on physical survival. His concepts and methodologies are essential in that they better prepare his clients to accept the realities of their situations while also greatly shorten the time necessary for them to achieve a whole and healthy relationship. It is Mr. Rosselot's hope that his books will also help eradicate the disease of divorce and family decay by providing the general public with these proven concepts that have worked for his clients for over 30 years.

DEDICATIONS

I dedicate this book to

SHIRLEY MARIE ROSSELOT,

my wife and very best friend.

During these fifty-four years that we

have been married, she has always

been there encouraging and supporting

me in ways that if stated would

fill volumes of books.

ACKNOWLEDGMENTS OF APPRECIATION

To women of all ages who found trust in me when in therapy. By sharing their most personal and intimate life experiences, they now contribute to other women who can benefit from learning that they can heal and go on with their lives when new understandings are achieved as written in this book. I also grew and learned more about my role as a man – especially, a deeper understanding of the complexity of women.

To my FOUR CHILDREN: Michael Rosselot, Miriam "Mim" Davis, Marsha Thomas, and Merrilee Spears. Their lives from birth to the present have inspired me to always be in touch with each moment life presents. Occasionally it took quite a bit of courage living with their creative inventiveness!

To my FRIENDS AND TEACHERS who have been a part of my life adding to these concepts, knowledge, insights, and my personal growth and development.

To my FATHER AND MOTHER: Glen and Grace Rosselot, who gave me a marvelous heritage and a very

ACKNOWLEDGMENTS

enriched exposure to life. They were missionaries in Sierra Leone, West Africa. My father was principal of the Albert Academy, a mission high school of 40 to 50 young men. Many of these men after World War II came to the United States for their advanced degrees and established careers resulting in worldwide contributions.

Some of these men include Dr. John Karefa Smart. He became Assistant General Counsel with the World Health Organization. I knew him when I was a boy and he was a student at the academy. We are still in contact with each other. He now lives with his wife Reena in Maryland. We talk and see each other often. Richard Caulker and his brother Soloman Caulker, Margi, and especially Warati and his wife Mary were a few of the individuals with whom I've been in contact over the years. Mary worked in our home when I lived at the Academy and took care of me as I grew up. Warati and Mary later married.

I don't want to overlook Bo-Bo, my childhood friend. Once he encouraged me to go without clothes as he did. Not wanting to be different, I immediately took off my clothes and continued to play. Later I went home without my clothes indicating that I was now a part of being an African little boy. My parents very kindly let Bo-Bo know

ACKNOWLEDGMENTS

that while it was all right for him not to wear clothes, George was still to wear his clothes. The memories of all the adventures I had in Africa with Bo-Bo are wonderful and priceless.

To my SISTER, Eleanor Laura Frances Luhman, who played a major role in my life. Growing up together in Freetown, Sierra Leone, we became very close and in tune with each other. I learned about girls/women from her, especially how to respect and treat them. She often indicates that I was the "good kid" and she got all the blame. She also reminded me that I was very mischievous, and that I always seemed to find a way to get by with it.

It took a team to help make this book a reality. I am especially grateful for the valuable early readings of the manuscript from Lane Lunn, a member of our Lafayette Presbyterian Church and a grant writer for Florida Medical Association. Lane took the time to type the first five chapters that I had dictated into a recorder. This was and always will be cherished by me as a gift. It immediately gave me the motivation to complete this book. She essentially "jump started" the writing of this book. I want to acknowledge and thank my youngest daughter Merrilee who also helped type the first draft of this manuscript.

ACKNOWLEDGMENTS

I'd like to give my thanks to Barbara Lineberry. Barbara provided excellent proofreading. Barbara has worked with visually impaired people for many years and has read and put many textbooks on tape. She has proofread and been editorial assistant for a variety of sources over the years. And thank you to my eldest daughter Mim for countless months of transcribing, editing, organizing, designing and publishing this book.

For general support I'd also like to recognize my colleagues who sent letters of endorsement and have encouraged me to write these concepts to share with others. Special thanks go to Reubin O'D. Askew, Governor of Florida (1971-1979), Representative Everett Kelly, Florida House of Representatives for 22 years, Dr. Robert Miles, Psychiatrist, and Donald R. Bardill, Ph.D., LPSY Professor Emeritus, Florida State University and the Past National President, American Association of Marriage and Family Therapists.

And again, to Shirley, my loving wife and eternal friend. Shirley has opened my eyes to understandings I would have never known were it not for her sharing and caring for me. Knowing her as a person and woman has been the primary source for my knowledge and insight

ACKNOWLEDGMENTS

regarding the nature of women. I learned from her what it really means to be "ONE WITH EACH OTHER." She is the GREATEST GIFT OF MY LIFE. She is TRULY GOD GIVEN!

And most importantly, I am thankful to the Almighty God, the Creator, who gave me wisdom, discernment and insights to share with others.

CHAPTER I

The Myth

WOMEN'S TRAUMAS

Women are responsible for a man's sexual arousal. At least this is what women are taught and have been made to believe. The belief is that a man would not have these sexual feelings without thinking sexually about a woman, looking at a magazine or movie with sexual content, or being in the presence of a woman. This is the myth, and society believes this myth as fact. This myth causes a woman to believe she must take care of the problem she has created, or say "No" in a manner not to offend a man's feelings or his ego.

Men also believe this myth. In the man's current social belief system, the woman is in fact responsible for his sexual arousal. This myth has been the basis for endless years of confusion, dysfunction, and in some cases serious trauma.

CHAPTER I

⊷⊶

THE SECRET

Nature is only interested in continuing all living things. Fertilization for the purpose of procreation is nature's primary role. Human beings are of the mammal species. The physiology for sexual functioning is opposite for female and male mammals. For example, if a female lion is disturbed in protecting her offspring, pursuing food for survival, or in an aggressive state, she is not willing to be sexually approached. The further fact is under anger and aggression, biophysically, she will not be able to be orgasmic which causes fertilization toward procreation. However, if the female lion is aggressively attacked and overpowered, she will experience a FEAR response which will cause her to be orgasmic, of which fertilization for nature's purpose of procreation will be the result.

If a male lion is aggressive and overpowers the female lion, he is able to accomplish ejaculation for fertilization toward procreation. If the male lion is driven off by the female lion, due to her aggressive attacks toward him, he will sit and wait or walk away and not approach the lioness.

In conclusion, biophysically, the female mammal can be sexually orgasmic under fear but not if she is angry or irritated. The reverse is true for the male mammal. He has difficulty functioning under fear, conversely, he can function sexually if aggressive or angry.

You are probably wondering what this has to do with human beings. Biophysically, a woman has difficulty or is not able to function sexually if she is upset, angry or in a protective mode. On the other hand, if a woman is frightened, due to being inappropriately touched, molested, flashed and or raped, she physically has a high probability of experiencing minor to major sexual feelings, even an orgasm. Women who are raped and fear for their life can also experience orgasmic response. This is strictly nature being triggered.

This phenomenon is prevalent in a situation such as date rape. The woman may be orgasmic if she is experiencing physical or even psycho-emotional fear. This response causes the attacker to believe she

CHAPTER I

"wanted it" thereby justifying his actions. The woman may also be confused by experiencing sexual feelings and mistakenly believe the same thing. Worse, she carries the responsibility and guilt of his actions.

In summary, if a man is angry, aggressive, and overpowers a woman physically and psychologically, he is able to be sexually aroused and can sexually function. The myth, as stated above, causes the man to believe that he is appropriately behaving and that the woman, due to her sexual responsiveness, believes that she in fact desired him and caused his behavior. So by touching, fondling, flashing, or raping a woman, causing her to have a sexual response, the male is encouraged to pursue the woman and also believes she was responsible for his actions. Under these conditions he is able to function. When a young or older adult male sexually molests a female child he often sees or senses that she has nipple hardness or goose bumps. He does not understand that her response is due to fear.

Yet, the reverse is also true. If a man is frightened or has fear of performance believing he will not be able to measure up to what he perceives is expected of him the strong likelihood is that he will not be able to function

THE MYTH

sexually. This is one of the reasons why women are taught in rape protection courses to become angry, yell fire, and move aggressively. Not only does this create confusion and uncertainty in the man, it will also prevent her from experiencing any sexual response. *(NOTE: If the male is psychotic he may still be able to sexually function even with her anger.)*

The bottom line is the female does not cause the male's sexual response.

I once had a client come to her session stating she was still in shock. She told me that a man had broken into her apartment. He entered her bedroom where she was sleeping telling her she had better get ready for great sex. She was so angry from being awakened that she spontaneously shouted that he better be good and he better have a "big one" or get lost! Due to her aggression he lost his sexual drive and ran out of the room. I explained to her what I have shared with you regarding this subject. Fortunately she did the best thing she could have done. It

CHAPTER I

was also fortunate that the man was not psychotic. Sick... Yes!

A male patient of mine in his 40's was concerned about his current inability to gain an erection. He had been happily married and had never had any difficulty before. His wife had died a few years earlier. He had dated and seldom had difficulty functioning. I asked him if he could tell me when this problem began. He said he was in a bar, which was not something he did very often. A young woman he thought to be about 30 years old approached him and said, "I understand that older is better. How about showing me? Your place or mine is OK by me." This intrigued him so much that he accepted her offer. Under the pressure to perform he was not able to function. Due to this experience he believed he now had a permanent problem! I explained the social myth to him. He was relieved, understanding that in fact his sexual dysfunction was caused by the fear that he may not be able to measure up.

A woman, on the other hand, who may be bitter, carry a grudge, or who is in the midst of upsetting and difficult times, yet cares deeply about the man in her life, may not feel any sexual desire. The anger, sometimes hidden, may be carried on for years. This may cause a woman to wonder why she is not able to become sexually aroused or may be uninterested in having any sexual relationship with the one she loves.

By knowing these concepts, and the fact her lack of sexual desire or dysfunction was caused by her anger and bitterness, even from past traumas in her life, it brings understanding and relieves the pressure of wondering if she will ever have healthy sexual desires and honest intimacy with her loved one. Instead, knowing this concept provides a new-found freedom and appreciation of who she is and once the sources of anger are discovered and treated, a healing begins as well as the positive intimate feelings toward the man she loves.

> Once a woman understands this myth the healing process begins. She can now like herself, be free, and make positive decisions in her own best interest and well-being.

CHAPTER II

Discovering the Secret

GUILT AND PUNISHMENT

Women do not know or understand the role that nature plays. Nor are they aware of the social myth that women cause the man's arousal. So most women, knowing they experienced sexual feelings when traumatized, keep this a private and deep secret! If the man is caught, accused, punished, and even sent to prison, the woman still feels responsible. The tragic result is that this mistaken belief causes a woman to carry guilt and to punish herself. She believes she does not deserve positive things in her life, especially a healthy "significant other" or marital relationship! Learning the correct facts changes this and the woman can now freely pursue positive relationships and a creative life.

CHAPTER II

THREE QUESTIONS

In my practice working with women I discovered that there are three questions that indicate whether a woman had been sexually invaded and to what degree.

Question #1: "Do you like yourself?" and "Have you always liked yourself?"

This is the first question I ask a woman to discover if she has been sexually traumatized. If she says she likes herself, I then ask if she has always liked herself. If she says, "No," I inquire when in her life she feels she did not like herself. I follow the question and have her share at what age and in what way she did not like herself.

She may say it was when she was between the ages of 12 and 13. Her concern at that time centered on whether she would be liked by her peers, especially other girls. She would continue and state how she felt ugly, was very withdrawn, shy and self-conscious around boys and men. She would mention that she felt she did not deserve nice things or friends, and often would stay home rather than become involved in activities. She would generally feel she was not worth anything. These would be her responses to not liking herself.

This gives an indication that she may have been sexually traumatized, especially if she states many of the reasons mentioned above. As trust is established she may be willing to indicate the actual traumatic event or events in her life.

Question #2: "Do you like your physical self?" and "Have you always liked your physical self?"

Sometimes the response is "Yes." The traumatized individual will usually hesitate and say, "Not really" or "NO!!" To the response of "Yes" it is important to ask if she has always liked her physical self. Often the individual will carefully pause and might respond that there have been times or a time when she did not like her physical self. I follow up this response by asking when she remembers not liking her physical self. Again, many times the answer is around 12 or 13 years old. This is a normal response with the primary concerns being physical development. Early adolescent girls are often concerned about their physical

CHAPTER II

development, especially in comparing themselves to other girls.

If the person answers using many negative illustrations the probability of being more severely sexually traumatized increases. Responses such as: "Between six and eight years old, I hated my body!" or "I often felt dirty and never liked to look at myself in the mirror, especially my body" or "I always wore clothes that covered my body and almost never wore dresses" or "I tried to avoid looking at or thinking about my body." Many times a specific age or age range is recalled as to when the dislike of her physical self began. The age she states indicates when the trauma took place in her life.

In the first question, certain responses regarding not liking herself may reveal possible sexual trauma(s). Additionally, if in the response to the second question, the person states she does not or has not liked her physical self, the degree of trauma is increased. Examples of these types of traumas could include being sexually stimulated by an older male touching her breasts, clitoral hand stimulation by a man, being encouraged to hand masturbate a male not in her age range, and being encouraged by a older male to watch pornography or vivid sexual films alone with him.

Question #3: "Do you have any significant memory gaps?"

Many times the woman will immediately state she has a very specific memory gap. She will also be able to indicate the time she cannot remember anything. If she is uncertain, the next step is to have her start with her earliest recollections and move chronologically through her life. This may reveal a memory gap of significance.

People who lived in the same home and location often have difficulty identifying chronological memory. Some approaches would be to have the person think about events at various grade levels, try to remember her house and its various rooms, have her think back to possible events related to meals, family activities, where she studied or had friends visit. Sometimes talking and remembering room colors, furniture arrangement and any special events centered around her family activities would open an opportunity to determine if there is a memory gap. If there are no significant memory gaps, this will most often indicate that the individual has not been traumatized in a major sexual invasion.

CHAPTER II

When the individual answers the first two questions, that she does not like herself now or in the past, plus does and or did not like her physical self, and answers the third question that a significant memory gap is uncovered or stated, the strong probability is she has experienced a major trauma. This could include being raped, forced to perform oral sex, date raped, anal sex, multiple rape by a group of males, or worse. The answer to these three questions indicate a major sexual invasion has happened to the woman.

Based on her response regarding any of the above questions I can help the woman realize the degree of sexual trauma she has experienced.

ADDITIONAL TRAUMA INDICATORS

Other indicators of sexual trauma to be considered are as follows:
- Choosing men who physically abuse her. In this case there is a high probability that she has been severely sexually traumatized.

- Choosing a man who is dominant, indifferent, a complainer, who manipulates her to be his caretaker, who has little or no relationship responsibility or work ethic and is seldom complimentary. This can reveal that the trauma was related to the first question of not liking herself.

- Choosing a man who verbally abuses her on a consistent basis, puts her down and complains that she is weak, stupid, and is only positive when he "wants sex." This can be an indication that the woman has answered the first two questions in a negative manner.

- Being angry with men and choosing a man she can dominate and attack his masculinity in an open or subtle way. This may also indicate she has been sexually traumatized.

(NOTE: These indicators can identify potential sexual trauma even if the first three questions have not been asked. Making any of these choices can reveal the possibility of historical sexual trauma even without pursuing therapy.)

CHAPTER III

Illustrations of Levels of Trauma

There are three levels of women's traumas. These are illustrations of the three levels that indicate the degrees of sexual abuse. The level is directly related to how a woman is currently feeling and how she values her life. In addition, the degree of trauma will influence the type of man she chooses in her life. The more severe the injury, the greater the probability the woman will choose a man who himself is injured. A man who is angry toward women will potentially search out the woman who has been traumatized. Of course, neither is aware that this is how it works. It seems that each will unconsciously see the other individual's trauma and injury. Both are highly attracted to each other, almost like two magnets.

Although a higher level of trauma means a longer process of healing and recovery, it is still liberating, and the process will still occur where the woman is set free from the guilt and she will begin the process of recovery and renewal.

CHAPTER III

Once a woman can understand the concepts in this book she immediately starts the healing process. She is able to explore her own life and move on to more positive choices and experiences. She will also be able to immediately tell if a male is angry or aggressive and will cease to choose that type of person. New processes and thinking occur and new choices are then made, good choices and healthier choices.

LEVEL ONE

I worked with a woman who could not think of herself in positive ways. She had a career, she enjoyed two wonderful children, she had many friends and as she put it, an "OK" husband. She rather quietly explained to me that she had very little sexual desire for her husband, but on occasion she could respond to him, basically taking care of his needs. She further stated she had difficulty having sexual feelings when touched physically.

I encouraged her to go back to early life experiences and explore if there had been any time in her

LEVELS OF TRAUMA

life where she had been touched inappropriately sexually. She said with a rather deep sigh, "yes," when she was around 11 or 12 an uncle had touched her breasts. I asked if she remembered having any sexual feelings. Rather reluctantly she indicated that she had felt her nipples get hard and began to blush and feel very strange inside. This was an uncle that she had highly respected, and felt that she had done something to cause him to touch her in this way.

I explained the myth and nature's role in a woman's sexual response and that she in fact did not cause her uncle to touch her even though she did have a sexual response, causing her to think she had created his behavior by some kind of action on her part. Once she understood that she was not the cause, she sat straight up and became very upset and enraged. She expressed her feelings of anger and disgust toward her uncle. This was the beginning of her being free and she had the ability to start the healing process using the concepts I mentioned. With this information she could now like herself and enjoy other people, family, friends, and children.

Another illustration is a 40-year-old woman who came to see me. In a very similar way she indicated

CHAPTER III

she had difficulty looking at herself in the mirror. She particularly had difficulty without any clothes on. She avoided any kind of clothes that would be feminine or would have any sexual suggestiveness to them. She was also somewhat overweight.

Again going through the same procedure, I asked her to go back to any recollection she had where she felt she had been inappropriately touched or sexually approached. She sat there for a little while and then shared that at one time she and a girlfriend of hers had been playing Frisbee outside in her girlfriend's backyard that was quite wooded. Her girlfriend threw the Frisbee way over her head and she ran back to get it which happened to be behind some bushes. As she bent down to pick up the Frisbee, she looked up and there was a man standing there who had been watching them. He had shed his clothes and began to fondle his genitals and smile at her. She stood there frozen for a moment, and then ran back screaming to her girlfriend who also ran back to see what she saw. The man was gone.

The belief, I explained to her, is that he would not have exposed himself had she not been a female. I helped her understand that she had perceived that she had done something to have this man expose himself to her. Again once she could understand that she did not cause this, even if she had feelings of some sexual rush, embarrassment, and, as she described it, "some goose bumps," she then could be free and realize that in fact she did not cause this event and she was not to blame. She said, "I feel so much better and I believe I can really begin to enjoy my life more."

These and other illustrations would be similar to what I would consider a level one sexual trauma.

LEVEL TWO

I worked with a young woman who indicated she had been inappropriately touched. She went on to tell me that when she was about 15 she had taken a shower and stepped out and reached for her towel when the door opened, and her stepfather was standing there. He walked toward her and took the towel from her and began to dry her off. As he did so he took his time touching special areas of her body that caused her to feel very strange and

CHAPTER III

actually have body response that she interpreted was sexual. She was shocked and couldn't believe that she was having any kind of response. He then dropped the towel and began to touch her further in a more intently sexual way, even to the point of touching her on her vagina, but not penetrating. He also massaged her breasts and her nipples became hard. She was so shocked that she could not scream, in fact, she knew it would do no good because her mother was out shopping, and she and her stepfather were home alone. He left the bathroom saying she was never to tell anyone what had happened.

The woman said I was the first person that she had ever shared her experience with. I gave her the information regarding the sexual myth and nature's role in a woman's sexual response. She stood up, looked out the window in almost disbelief and said, "I didn't do anything to have him do that to me? I didn't cause it! He's a sick man, isn't he?" I said, "I think that goes without saying." She said, "I want to know more about those things you talked about in terms of what I can do to once again really like myself and enjoy my life." She also indicated that she wanted to bring her husband into therapy and try to help him understand her responses where possibly she could begin to have a fulfilling marriage.

When I explained that women choose men who have also been injured, she said "It would be helpful to have him understand his level of injury so that he can also be all right. Then the two of us could be happy and enjoy our lives in wonderful and fulfilling ways." I shared with her that her depression was really oppression. Sometimes when people are oppressed and have been forced to do something against their will, they feel that it was their fault. Since they feel that they could not do anything about a particular situation, they becoming depressed. She was not clinically depressed; her depression was a result of oppression based on what had happened to her.

LEVEL THREE

I am sure that you have by now anticipated that each level would be more severe. In this level the woman chooses a more aggressive and angry male even though initially he may not appear to be so. I had been working with an individual for five or six sessions regarding various issues in her life related to career decisions, difficulty making decisions, what to buy at the grocery store, even deciding to go to the grocery store or go out and be with

CHAPTER III

other people. She said that many times she would just stay at home and do nothing, read a book or do something just to take up the time. She shared with me that at the present time she was in a very difficult relationship with a man five years older, she being in her 30's. I asked her what she meant by difficult and she said "Well, he basically had a lot of potential and I could see that he would really be someone with whom I could have a good relationship. However, he is quite dominant and wants his own way and many times puts me down." He often blamed her for things she felt she was not responsible for, believing she had done nothing to cause his him to get upset.

I asked her if he had ever been physically abusive toward her. She said "I hoped you wouldn't ask me that. Is this a confidential situation?" I assured her it was confidential with the one condition that if there was any indication of imminent or major possibility of harm to where her life was in danger, then it would be necessary for me by law and ethics to report that to the authorities and help her remove herself from the situation. She understood that and felt she could trust me and we could work together. She indicated if there were any danger she would report it immediately.

She said on occasion he would push her and sometimes hit her if he felt she wasn't responding to him the way he liked. She indicated that there were times he was particularly sexually aggressive toward her. At that point she hesitated and said "What I can't understand is that sometimes when he's sexually aggressive I experience a high sexual peak even at the point of having an orgasm." She said it had always puzzled her that this could happen under that type of situation. She said, "I thought that type of response only came when it was a kind, caring, loving, intimate situation." She went on to say that in the past when she had a relationship that was kind and loving, she basically had little feelings of sexual desire and often would have some feeling but not really complete sexual response.

I shared with her that there was a high possibility at some point in her life, consciously or unconsciously, she had been severely sexually abused before she was 18 or 20. She said she couldn't really recall any major situations of that kind. I asked her if she had any primary memory gaps in her life and she said that she had, somewhere between the ages of 14 and 16. She could recall very few things even if she would go back and trace actions or activities. We tried to go back and trace things like where she lived, where she remembered her room to be, family members,

CHAPTER III

and so forth. She had very few and very vague memories during that period of time. She indicated it almost took looking at pictures or photographs to give her some kind of recall.

I then asked her if she liked herself and she responded not really. I also asked her if she liked her physical self and she said, "Who would want to do that? What do you mean?" I said, "Well, do you like your body?" She said, "No, I can't even look at my body." I shared with her the high possibility that she had been sexually traumatized during that period of time in her life in a major way and that she had blocked it out in order for self-protection to take place.

She sat there for a while, and then tears began to flow. She said, "I think I know what it might have been." I sat and waited for her response, which took 15 or 20 minutes. She indicated that at one time she was in a car with two young men, one was somewhat older, and the other about her same age. The older boy was about 19, close to 20. She said that they, without her realizing it, had driven out into the country and had gone on a back road where they stopped the car. She inquired what was going on and they said "Well, its time. You're such a wonderful, sexy girl that we know that you want it." She said she was stunned and didn't know what to do. She said they pulled her out of the car and undressed her. She was shocked and frightened. Both the boys raped her and molested her in many different ways including insisting on oral sex.

After sharing this memory, she just sat there. I asked her "Do you remember experiencing any physical response even though I'm sure you think this is a very strange question?" She said "I don't know why you asked me that, but what has puzzled me all these years is that I actually came, you know, I actually had an orgasm." Once we talked about the concept I have been sharing in this book, she realized the fact that physically being sexually responsive was strictly nature due to her fear and she didn't cause the aggression. She sat there in shock. She then stood up and said "All these years I thought it was my fault! I know those boys, now men, are getting off scott free. I'm going to do something about it!"

We talked about what she might do that would be in her best interest. For example, she could find things she liked about herself, causing healing, instead of acting out of retribution. She said "You know, that's a good point." She

CHAPTER III

went on to say "I really think something needs to be done because these men may have hurt other girls or women and it needs to stop. I'm going to really think about it and see what the alternatives are at this point and talk to an attorney." She then asked if I would continue to work with her and I agreed.

I was also working with a woman who was in her late 20's. She had an older brother who was eight years older than she. We had worked together in therapy for sometime. Once when she came in she said "I really trust you and want to share something with you that has been upsetting to me for a long time." She then shared with me that from the time she was about 12 years old her older brother had been sexual with her even to the point of intercourse. She said hesitantly, "He was concerned that when I got a little older I could get pregnant and therefore he should wear a condom." She said "He also manipulated me to be sexual with him in different ways, oral sex and by hand, etc." She said that this went on for many years until he left the house. When she became 18 she also left. Even on occasion, after she moved out, he would try to see her. She looked at me to see what my reaction would be.

Then she said, "Why did I let him do that all that time?" I shared with her again the myth and nature's role. She shared immediately with me that yes, she was constantly frightened of him and afraid that when he would approach her he would involve her in sexual activities. After hearing my explanation, she was relieved and sat back in her chair breathing easily. She then began to exclaim how she hated her brother, how he was terrible, sick and mean and had always given her the feeling that she was to blame causing his sexual approaches. She said she sees him rarely now, she can go on with her life knowing that he's the one that has deep severe problems, and that she can now heal and be herself. She shared that she had other experiences where she seemed to pick men who were abusive, and one in particular had been physically abusive toward her.

Since her discovery of her past and the new knowledge of these concepts, dispelling the myth and revealing the secret, she realized that it had been a while since she'd seen her brother and she was no longer interested in or bound by that secret or that relationship.

CHAPTER IV

The Result

OPPRESSION

When a woman is sexually traumatized she experiences extreme feelings of loss and low self esteem. Trauma is oppressive which places the person in a state of depression. Many times I find that an individual is treated for depression only pharmacologically without psychotherapy. Psychotherapy would explore possible traumas, loss issues or life being oppressive, past or present. The results of oppression are:

- FIGHT
- FLIGHT
- WITHDRAW

Fight is the first attempt to find ways to overcome what is oppressive. These behaviors can range from verbal to physical aggression. If that is not successful the next step is to flee the oppressor or what is causing the oppression. Flight can be daydreaming, avoiding possible difficult situations more than usual, or actually leaving the scene. If the first two steps do not relieve the oppression, the next and most severe state is to withdraw. Many times women isolate themselves, limit friendships, and are afraid to venture beyond their residence. They can often become agoraphobic.

Once an individual is receiving therapy, new coping skills can be learned that will help resolve oppression. In addition, there are anti-depressive and anti-anxiety medications that can help while an individual is gaining insights and understanding in therapy.

GRIEF

Upon discovery, realizing and understanding all that has created the damaging trauma, there is a period of grief that a woman will experience. Although she may have grieved over past events, now it is a grief over the discovery, the awareness, the loss of time and happiness. Most often grief is a primary factor to be dealt with gently. It takes time to move through the stages of grief, plus there are situations where a person remains in a certain stage for many years. There are five stages of grief:

1. SHOCK ~ DENIAL
2. ANGER
3. PLATEAU
4. SETTING NEW GOALS
5. RESOLUTION

Shock often results in denial. The individual feels and often states, "Why me? I can't believe this is happening to me. Why was I picked to be traumatized? I just can't believe it and I never will." All of these thoughts and feelings and similar feelings are indicators of shock. It may even be more frustrating to realize that there are not always answers. It may be difficult to acknowledge that being traumatized was not the individual's fault. Denials and shock will occur over a period of time. Once this is realized, the next stage of grief is anger.

Anger is a by-product of many symptoms such as: being physically and/or emotionally harmed, ridiculed, mocked, teased, scorned, verbally or physically abused,

CHAPTER IV

devalued, excluded, insulted, and of course invaded sexually against one's will. It is very important to help the person to identify her anger and be able to express her feelings now knowing she no longer needs to carry guilt. Writing about feelings and drawing, as in art therapy, can help her to acknowledge that her traumas and issues are due to the other individual's problems.

Plateau is a time period when a woman integrates the discoveries from shock and anger into her present healing mental state. As integration progresses, new goals can be developed. A primary consideration is that the individual clearly understands and believes the myth and nature's role, plus utilizing the new healing tools both physical and emotional. She will come to the realization that she was not the cause of the tragedy and will actively shift into a new place emotionally. This will move her into the next state where she will automatically set new goals for herself. Indicators are increased self-esteem, self-confidence, enjoying life in general, making positive career decisions, and wanting to move forward in her life. One observable result by the individual and others will be her choice of a more appropriate significant man, if this is her desire.

THE RESULT

One other way to help a woman understand what to learn about men is to find out what a man was like growing up. She should find out what kind of home life he had, and if he had any kind of traumas, particularly a harsh father or being put down by his mother, or physically abused by his father, stepfather or any other adult males in the family system.

Setting new goals may range from choosing a new career, changing a job from where she is unhappy to pursuing new training which enhances her life. One of the primary indicators of healing would be that she feels she deserves good things and positive relationships. Once new goals are activated and in place, resolution occurs automatically.

> **Overcoming grief sets the stage for the individual to add on to her life and live creatively!**

CHAPTER V

The Obsession
MEN'S TRAUMAS

The concepts in this book would not be complete if I did not address the issues of traumas experienced by men. The question is "Are men also traumatized? If so, in what ways?"

Yes, men and boys are also traumatized, however, we tend to use the word injured. Men are injured in different ways. The type of injury produces different effects. The outcome will show itself in the primary relationship he has with a woman, particularly once married. This is a subject in and of itself related to men's injuries.

The core problem is that the injured male is attracted to the traumatized female in the same way as the traumatized female is attracted to the injured male. This is especially true when the attraction is primarily

CHAPTER V

physical and sexual. The physical/sexual attraction is more prominent than the emotional/personal attraction by which the individuals choose each other.

Strong sexual response that includes female fear and male aggression increases the degree by which each person was traumatized/injured. Often the injured male has difficulty ejaculating. This male has little or no regard for the woman as a person. He feels the female sexually responding to him believes she wanted him even though she may say "No, don't!!" These angry men are seldom attracted to women who have had no sexual injury.

> *(NOTE: If the male is pathogenic or psychotic then the anger/fear factor does not apply, and that male can function and will pursue a female whether she has been traumatized or not.)*

Individuals who are not traumatized/injured are attracted to each other for a balance of all their personal qualities beyond just predominantly sexual. The sexual feelings are not the underlying primary reason to pursue or be attracted to the opposite gender. Healthy individuals can achieve positive sexual experiences. The injured/

traumatized individuals often perceive that they are attracted to the other. However, their primary drive is related to the historical trauma or injury that creates a very intense sexual connection between them.

There seems to be a paradox. The greater the sexual desire and attraction, the greater the potential that the woman has been traumatized. When this intense sexual desire and attraction occurs the high probability is that she has chosen a man who has been injured. Of course this can be confusing because people do have attraction for each other that involve feelings of sexual arousal, which is normal. The difference is in the degree, intensity, and that the sexual feelings are predominant and maintain themselves as the primary reason for the relationship. The sexual attraction overrides the dynamics of an interpersonal relationship that includes love, caring and wanting to share with each other their values beyond the purpose that the end result will be a sexual encounter.

As explained, when a woman's primary attraction is sexual it is nature playing a predominant role in her desire, especially if she has been traumatized in her life sexually. An additional problem is that the traumatized woman often has a sense of low self-esteem and self-worth.

CHAPTER V

Men as well as women believe the myth that women cause men's sexual arousal. A common term is "turn on". She "turns him on" by her look, her walk, her voice or how she dresses and other feminine characteristics.

The myth supports men's obsession. As a little boy matures he begins to have wet dreams, erections, and sexual feelings. These are associated with thoughts of girls in all kind of fantasies. It's further reinforced as he develops relationships with girls. It's well known that children involve themselves in show and tell. It is very normal for males to experience erection physiologically without thinking about or seeing a female. Men have been programmed with the belief that if they experience an erection there should be a vagina available. This implies many missed opportunities.

The historical moral and spiritual codes state that sexual intercourse is only appropriate once married. This implies that sexual feelings need to be suppressed and not acted upon until one is married. This belief actually accelerates the obsession. To tell someone not to think about something essentially makes them think more about it. This is especially true if you say "don't." The word "don't" in our minds means "do." When a parent tells a teenager "don't come in later than 9:00" even a well-behaved child will stroll in ten minutes or hours late.

Our society also contributes to men's obsessions. Magazines such as Playboy and Penthouse graphically illustrate the female body. These and other magazines carry many articles with sexual content most often catering to the male's libido. Movies, books, and our general social environment give credence to the fact that women are responsible for a male's sexual desire and arousal.

When you put the normal sexual functioning of a male together with the woman's social myth it creates the male's obsessive nature. It's almost as though he cannot stop his sexual arousal when he sees, thinks or fantasies about a woman. It's like the "pop ups" on a computer screen.

CHAPTER V

THE ANTIDOTE

Men must change the mistaken belief that they must have a woman when aroused. Rather, go beyond this single-mindedness and see a woman as a person and get to know her as a person, not just as an object. The magnetic attraction or "attraction felt from across a room" may not occur, but instead a more complete pleasure-bond can be realized with a woman.

The man believes that society says you must take care of 'it' – your physical needs – that if you aren't taking care of it, you are missing out, you are not man enough, or you are not complete. This is not the same fulfillment that can be achieved through concentrating on a true friendship – two people choosing life together. Discovering the wonderful things about the person, the whole person will help a man relax more, be less dependent on simple sexual gratification, and desire the development and discovery of a woman and an interpersonal relationship.

Men need to be taught to see a woman as a whole person. Every person has mental, emotional, physical, social-cultural, and spiritual resources. The physical nature of a human being is only one element of the total person. Exploring all five of these resources eliminates obsessing over one area. Any obsession is harmful to an individual whether it's gambling, alcohol, drugs, food, sex, fitness, and even the Internet. A healthy life is made up of balance. A book *The Vital Balance* written by Karl Menninger and Martin Mayman, gives many concepts for developing a complete life.

> **Men need to be taught to see a woman as a whole person.**

CHAPTER VI

The Recovery

HEALING APPROACHES

Be Aware of the Myth

I have found that it is not necessary to have a person relive the trauma in order to heal and resolve the injury. When I share the myth that a woman causes a man's sexual arousal plus nature's role where under fear, biologically, a woman can experience sexual responses, the person will say or exclaim, "All these years I have believed it was my fault! You mean it wasn't my fault after all?" Very often the person breaks into tears or just sits in disbelief. This awareness is the first step toward healing.

CHAPTER VI

Employ Positive Options

Discussing the positive or negative outcomes of pursuing the perpetrator is another healing approach if the individual has not been confronted in her past. It seems that when the perpetrator was not revealed, caught and punished, the woman does not seem to carry as much guilt or self-punishment. The woman's attitude and behavior still exhibits the results of sexual trauma. By reviewing options in how to deal with the traumatizer, it opens opportunities to act and move in positive steps or to choose not to act but instead resolve her need for closure.

I encourage the person to give herself "Yes's and "No's". Essentially this means to say yes to choose things that are positive for her and say no to things she feels are not in her best interest. This is not to encourage narcissism. In fact sometimes narcissistic behavior can also indicate trauma or being over indulged as a child. By concentrating on positive behavior and activities the wounds will heal and be replaced by a renewing sense of self-worth.

Sometimes doing activities that are more personally fulfilling creates a healthy "me attitude" and starts opening opportunities to rejoin society and in turn to get involved in life. Helping others is healing and improves self esteem as well. Ideas such as buying that set of earrings, a new dress, starting a hobby, developing new friends, going to the gym, having a manicure she has been putting off, a new hair style, exploring new interests, and encouraging her significant other to join with her in couples therapy.

Also, it is important to mention that individual therapy for a person can be a positive step toward healing and resolution. Although this book provides concepts that give new insights ~ it may also be a beginning step to reveal the need for additional professional counseling.

Know That We Are Unique, Individual Miracles

In another healing approach, sharing that she is a miracle, a one of a kind, helps her to acknowledge her uniqueness as a person. God created human beings in His own image with all of His abilities and talents. The wonderful fact about this Creator is that He knew marvelous psychological/physical principles. He set everything in place for us to discover. Rather than doing

CHAPTER VI

everything for us or giving us everything on a silver platter, He knew that the joy of building self-esteem is to discover answers for ourselves. When anything new is discovered a person can say, "Look what I can do!" or "Look what I found!" Yes, sometimes the discovery is confusing or not what we had hoped for, but there are answers that can be pursued. This God, this Master Creator, is not like the Greek or Roman mythological gods who played with human beings as puppets. Rather this is the God who is the Creator of the universe, the earth, all of mankind. Each individual is a miracle and a "one-of-a-kind". The very recent scientific discoveries regarding the human DNA can trace genetic lines for millions of years. We are each unique and wondrously made.

The Judeo-Christian scriptures state that God created the world in seven days. This can be interpreted as seven ages, which allows for billions of years, as we know time. I think of cybernetics as further indication of being a miracle. During World War II the technical discoveries grew in quantum leaps. Cybernetics brought into focus that the greatest engineering phenomenon is the human physical body.

THE RECOVERY

The brain is studied to invent technical communication systems as complex as computers, cell phones, etc. Artificial intelligence is being worked on as I write this book. It has still not been achieved to where a computer can think for itself. (My concern is who and what values will be used for that system!!!) At this time a machine has not been invented that can give birth to itself and by itself, neither has a computer system been made to program itself creating its own software. Yes, there may be advances held highly secret of which most of us are unaware, and is beyond our imagination, except for Science Fiction.

The human joint system is researched and copied to build cranes and lifting systems both large and small. The human muscle system is studied to develop materials to pull, push or hold any object. The skin is studied to develop materials needed to cover many objects. Materials having the ability to expand and contract without cracking, plus the ability to deal with temperature changes are characteristics of the human skin. The

> Each person is unique and wondrously made ~ you are a miracle to behold!

CHAPTER VI

ability of the skin to peel and replace itself is also studied and copied. I was once told that the heat shield of a space capsule is designed after the skin. If a solid material were to be used it might heat up and radiate back, burn up the capsule and the astronaut. Material with many layers to peal off upon re-entering the atmosphere would not radiate which protects the capsule and astronauts.

The veins and arteries are studied for their ability to expand, contract and contain valves that do not permit blood and other bodily fluids to flow backward. The heart is the most complex pump. The cells inside the human mouth constantly replace themselves. If a person bites his inner cheek the cells are replaced without scar tissues. If this were not true, by the time a person was three to five years old he/she would have difficulty talking due to all the scar tissue, from accidentally biting his/her inner cheek.

Did you know that a woman's vagina is made of cells that replace themselves? The vagina is renewed each month a woman has her menstrual cycle. This is an incredible refreshing and renewal and an example of how wonderfully the body is made. One additional fact of significance is that the human body is made up of atomic and subatomic elements. We are not solid as it appears.

The additional miracle is that every cellular system is made up of atomic and subatomic elements that are totally regenerated every seven years on average.

When all of the above information is shared with a woman, citing these many examples, she learns how she is a miracle and that she a beautiful creation! With the skin, vagina, and even the tissue in a person's mouth constantly being replaced it means a person, especially a woman, is constantly brand new! This body renewal also applies to men.

Experience the Renewal

It's true that the memory of any sexual trauma remains and needs healing, but a woman now understands that she is physically renewed since the body has discarded any physical invasion. (The exception to this would be sexually transmitted diseases or external scars and disfigurations not able to be resolved by plastic surgery.) Wonderfully, the body's atomic and subatomic system is still being constantly renewed.

CHAPTER VI

Once the person understands and has time to integrate this new knowledge, I suggest the following steps which will begin the mental/emotional healing as the woman experiences pleasurable feelings, thoughts and actions.

- She can find time to spend renewing the feelings of being physically new. One way is by taking a long bath using any desired bath oils and enjoying the warmth and pleasure of the bath. If comfortable about it, she can slowly and tenderly touch her body reminding herself that she is brand new. Place a Do Not Disturb sign outside the door so there are no interferences during this personal time.

- She may want to give herself a manicure, read, listen to beautiful music, start a hobby, explore new interests, do imaginative activities such as creative writing, painting or drawing, or writing songs for healing.

- Exercise, physical activity helps with being emotionally and mentally fit. As stated in the *Mental Health Journal,* "There is a growing body of work demonstrating that exercise promotes wellness and mental health. Researchers at Duke University studied people suffering from depression for 4 months and found that 60% of the participants who exercised for 30 minutes three times a week overcame their depression without using antidepressant medication." In addition, it increases circulation, provides renewed strength, vitality and emotional clarity.

- Invest consistent and quality time in meditation and spiritual renewal. Finding a private place, playing soft quiet music to study, reflect, meditate and pray will provide spiritual and emotional centering. During this time she can think or say aloud statements such as:

    - *I am a worthwhile person.*
    - *I am a miracle.*
    - *I have many wonderful attributes (and state them).*
    - *Each day I am going to love and know myself more.*
    - *I have unlimited potential.*
    - *I am renewed.*
    - *I am going to add on to my life by making lists of positive things I am going to choose to do.*

CHAPTER VII

The New Vision

LOVE

Love is a wonderful word that has many meanings and dynamics. We are socially taught that a person is not to think of oneself; to do so is to potentially be self-centered and again narcissistic.

A wonderful man who lived two thousand years ago, in my opinion, set the foundation for holistic psychology. He told those living then, which still applies now, to "Love thy neighbor as thyself." Yes, it is very important to love your neighbor. The emphasis is usually placed on "Thy neighbor." In order to love others it is important and necessary to love yourself.

CHAPTER VII

Think of a wonderful spring that sends forth gallons of clear fresh water. It flows forming a river causing the earth to flourish and provides clear, fresh water for animals and human beings to drink. Fish, frogs, and plants all thrive in the water. Human beings benefit from the clear water by drinking, swimming, boating and enjoying nature in all its marvel and beauty.

What a different world it would be if every human being believed they were like a wonderful flowing spring, contributing to others and to the world in ways that cause life to flourish. To be more conclusive, the more a person can grow, the greater the contribution. One additional thought is when a person visualizes contributing in creative meaningful ways, the result will be to not allow any "junk" to enter into their physical or emotional life. When a traumatized woman views herself as a wonderful flowing clear spring increased healing takes place.

One of the most descriptive illustrations of love is found is in the Bible in I Corinthians, Chapter 13, starting with Verse 4. It states in *The New English Bible:*

> "Love is patient; love is kind and envies no one. Love is never boastful, nor conceited, nor rude; never selfish, not quick to take offence. Love keeps no score of wrongs; does not gloat over other men's sins, but delights in the truth. There is nothing love cannot face; there is not limit to its faith, its hope, and its endurance."

Many times an attempt is made to determine who is loved the most. This is most often found in families. The truth is that everyone is a FIRST. Each individual needs to be loved as a unique, one-of-a-kind miracle. It is true that a person can be loved, but not liked due to various reasons which reaches into human values.

Ultimate love is to be freely chosen and to be able to freely choose with no coercion, manipulation, pressure, or bribery. Once again the Creator I have mentioned set in motion the most magnificent concept of Love that I have experienced.

CHAPTER VII

Being somewhat of a creative person, the following is *my* interpretation, of this concept:

"In the beginning of time, the Creator was alone and felt lonely. One day he decided to use his creative powers. He spoke the WORD, snapped his fingers, and a galaxy was created with infinite galaxies, stars, moons, and suns. He then thought and decided to create the Earth, which He did. He was still not satisfied so he decided to create oceans, mountains, plants, and to populate the earth. He added animals, fish, birds and creatures of all kinds! He was still lonely. He decided to create a Being "In His own Image," having all the creative abilities He possessed. He created man and woman. He was still contemplative and the most marvelous decision made by a Creator was to choose to give man and woman the option to FREELY CHOOSE to love Him. Herein lies the ultimate concept of Love! It is often called "Free Will." This meant that the Creator knew that to be truly Loved was to be freely chosen to be loved. God loves us unconditionally. This is Ultimate Love!! He went one step further. He let man and woman know that He would love them so much that it would be difficult for them to choose not to love Him."

FRIENDSHIP

There is a problem that develops when a traumatized women heals. She is conditioned to have sexual attraction and desire under a situation involving conscious or unconscious fear, as I have already explained. Once this person no longer is controlled by her historical trauma she may have difficulty sexually desiring another individual. She will now need to learn new responses that include attraction and desire that are based on a different set of principles and understandings that are not dependent on the historical trauma.

The woman can now experience attraction and desire through tender love, caring, sharing and relating in many beautiful ways with a man beyond the sexual interaction and attraction. That does not mean that the sexual attraction is not present in healthy individuals. Individuals who have not been traumatized/injured have a broader base for relating and being attracted to each other then just the sexual attraction itself. Thus the paradox, a woman may have a sexual attraction for a

CHAPTER VII

man whom she believes is good. If the sexual attraction is the predominant factor in her desire, she unknowingly chooses men who are basically angry/injured. She may feel that she is in love and highly attracted to him. In this manner the thought that is generally a normal belief of attraction can have an outcome of trauma. Once a woman understands these things and heals she no longer makes that choice and is free.

When a woman who has been traumatized understands what I have been sharing she goes through the steps to heal, often experiencing confusion. Since her desire formerly was based on the historical myths, she needs to restructure her conscious and unconscious conceptual framework that causes sexual desire. The wonderful thing is that once a woman heals, she is no longer dependent upon the historical trauma to generate her sexual desires. She is now free to establish a whole new set of insights and understandings that can be more fulfilling in every way for her as a woman. She is now able to be a whole person and have experiences in all forms including beautiful sexual feelings. She can now involve herself in a whole set of new activities that will enhance her life and add to her as a woman and unique individual. She no longer needs to depend on a male to feel attractive and desirable and of worth. She can now establish relationships on the concept of two interdependent people choosing each other, with a balance of giving and receiving pleasures toward creative outcomes. It is a WITH rather than TO or FOR. TO or FOR denotes a dependency relationship.

Masters and Johnson in their research on human sexuality discovered this concept of two people choosing each other as two interdependent people being willing to relate to one another as individuals. This is as opposed to being dependent on the fact that the other individual has to be a certain way or perform a certain way. It is actually two people negotiating with each other toward a very positive relationship in every way. They are giving and receiving pleasure whether it be laughing, sharing, playing, touching, traveling, inventing things, and creating many forms of interaction between each other.

Think for a minute. If you had a chance to go on your dream vacation and it was completely paid for, you more than likely would try to see and do everything on the vacation that was possible. This could include sightseeing, dining, boating, skiing, or anything you love doing. The weather is perfect, the scenery is just the way you dreamed it and you have people or the person you enjoy around you

CHAPTER VII

to share this wonderful experience. Now picture taking this vacation and having to stay in your hotel room the entire time. You would never be able to experience and enjoy all of the resources the dream vacation had to offer. This is the same scenario with regard to a relationship between a woman and a man. By sharing and learning all that there is to know about each other, as individual miracles, with all each has to offer, a total fulfillment that is healthy, beautiful and exponential is available to experience. A woman, simply stated, is like the grandeur of an ocean. She is all the miracles within it to be explored and experienced.

> **When you think of each person as a miracle and then when two miracles come together using their entire God given resources, their potential is unlimited!**

As human beings we have five primary resources: mental, emotional, social/cultural, physical, and spiritual. These are the areas for people to explore within themselves. Two people exploring these five resources and choosing to share and explore these same resources with each other can create a very wonderful, synergetic relationship for a lifetime. Were people to realize this approach to a relationship it could certainly reduce the current 80% of people who find themselves divorced today. It would also markedly reduce domestic violence. With this new knowledge, opportunities for fulfilling life expand for each individual and the couple in quantum leaps and multidimensional ways. It is like two friends where what one person can't think of the other one can thus having a greater ability to explore life together in every possible way.

Let's build on the concept of exploring our unlimited resources as human beings. The one primary resource is our spiritual nature. The Creator gave us a gift of every possible resource that is in His possession and ability to give. Yes, we are MIRACLES!! God created us in His image. This is one of the most marvelous concepts that a person can imagine.

CHAPTER VIII

The Conclusion

In over 30 years of practice, I have worked with hundreds of women in this situation. It is true that over 95% of the traumatized women I have counseled were liberated and healed of hurts and the related consequences by simply hearing and understanding these basic principles and knowing about the myth and nature's role a woman holds as a secret. They no longer punish themselves. They cease to pick men that hurt them, they start loving themselves, and feeling good about who they are. Women have new insights and realize their attractions are due to prior traumas – this new knowledge or "ah ha" experience corrects their internal beliefs. As simple as the concept seems, this provides freedom from their emotional bondage. It truly creates a new way and a new life.

The woman is not to blame. Even more so, the healing is permanent. It provides healing for the rest of

CHAPTER VIII

their lives. They are no longer trapped by the myth and the secret ... they are now free to explore and enjoy their lives in every aspect with unlimited potential.

It is my hope that by helping individuals heal by learning this new knowledge will be a step to overcoming the pain in our society. My purpose in writing this book is to be able to help people stop hurting and start healing because they have learned about the myth and the secret and through this understanding have a fresh insight. These concepts, which seem simple in explanation, yet are complex in their totality, will help individuals to be free, to move forward and to explore a wonderful, beautiful life for themselves.

One human being is a marvelous miracle with infinite potential. Two people _with_ each other exploring and being explored can overcome the myth, the secret, and the obsession.

APPENDIX I

Supplemental Reading

SPECIAL SCRIPTURES

Scriptures for reflection, meditation and encouragement *(taken from the New American Standard Bible)*:

- Genesis 1:26-27
- Job 5:8-11
- Psalms 118:1
- Psalms 119:73
- Psalms 121
- Psalms 139:14-18
- Psalms 147:3,5
- Isaiah 41:10
- Lamentations 3:21-25
- John 3:16
- John 14:27
- Romans 12:2
- I Corinthians 13
- Philippians 4:6-8
- II Thessalonians 2:16-17
- I Peter 5:7

APPENDIX II

Resources

The following books are what I recommend as additional resources to help a woman improve her self-worth and to heal:

"Celebrate Yourself"
> Briggs, Dorothy. *Celebrate Yourself: Enhancing Your Self-Esteem*. Main Street Books, 1986.

"For Yourself"
> Barbach, Lonnie. *For Yourself: The Fulfillment of Female Sexuality*. Signet, 2000.

"Gift From The Sea"
> Lindbergh, Anne Morrow. *Gift From the Sea*. Vintage Books, 1978.

"Living A Beautiful Life"
> Stoddard, Alexandra. *Living a Beautiful Life*. Collins, 1988.

"Smart Cookies Don't Crumble"
> Friedman, Sonya. *Smart Cookies Don't Crumble: A Modern Women's Guide to Living and Loving Her Own Life*. Putnam Pub Group, 1985.

"Women's Reality"
> Shaef, Anne Wilson. *Women's Reality: An Emerging Female System*. Harper San Francisco, 1992.

"The Vital Balance"
> Menninger, Karl. *The Vital Balance: The Life Process in Mental Health and Illness*. Peter Smith Publisher, 1983.

"The Courage to Heal"
> Bass, Ellen and Davis, Laura. *The Courage to Heal: A Guide for Women Survivors of Child Sexual Abuse*. Harper Perennial, 1988.

APPENDIX III

About the Author
GEORGE FRANKLIN ROSSELOT

OVERVIEW

Professional Work Experience:

Founder, Owner and Executive Director of Eastwood Clinic, Inc., Tallahassee, Florida, with a full-time private practice as a Marriage and Family Therapist from 1973-2004. Director and Associate Professor at Florida A&M University and Director of Upward Bound, which targeted high-risk and high potential students who were underachievers from 1969-1974. Experience includes over 50 years of working in the areas of private practice, guidance counseling, education, social services, youth programs and ministry. In addition, Mr. Rosselot produced and hosted television programs in Tallahassee and Cleveland that dealt with social problems confronting adolescents and young adults.

APPENDIX III

Education:

M.S. Education, University of Akron; Post-Graduate work at Kent State University; B.S. Education, Indianapolis University; Doctoral course work and residency requirements fulfilled in Adult Education and Marriage and Family Therapy, Florida State University. Pastoral Theology course work at United Theological Seminary.

Clinical Experience:

Individual, Marriage and Family, Adolescent Psychotherapy, Divorce and Mediation Therapy, Rehabilitation and Career Counseling, Youth Ministry and Theological Counseling, Educational Television Production, Educational Consulting.

Professional Affiliations:

American Association of Marriage and Family Therapy, Past President of Florida Association of Marriage and Family Therapy, American Counseling Association, Florida Mental Health Counseling Association, American Association of Sex Educators, Counselors, and Therapists.

ABOUT THE AUTHOR

Licenses Held:

Licensed Marriage and Family Therapist, State of Florida: MT 0000001; Licensed School Psychologist, State of Florida: SS 0000049; Licensed Mental Health Counselor, State of Florida: MH 0000202.

Areas of Special Interest:

Marriage and Family Therapy, Adolescent and Young Adult Therapy, Gender Identity Issues; Human Sexuality and Education Counseling, Women's Trauras, Career and Psycho-Educational Consulting, Divorce Adjustment, Parent Education, Grief Therapy, Consulting in Organizational Systems, Spiritual Life Development.

Personal Background:

George Rosselot was born in Kokomo, Indiana in 1931. He was reared in Sierra Leone, West Africa. His parents were missionaries in West Africa until 1939 when the family returned to the State of Indiana. Mr. Rosselot has maintained personal relationships to this day with African leaders and friends. In addition to his illustrious career,

APPENDIX III

he also pioneered in over 15 extensive Youth Educational Study Trips which spanned a period of nine years. The experience included extensive travel throughout the United States. This program included working with a diverse group of individuals and ethnic organizations as well as various religious groups and cultures.

Current Information:

Mr. Rosselot is currently semi-retired and living with his wife of 54 years, Shirley M. Rosselot. They reside in Tallahassee, Florida and have four children, three grandchildren, and three great-grand children. In his own words he has not retired, rather, he has "re-wired" and is now engaged in writing and publishing several books that have been in development over the past 30 years from concepts developed through his clinical therapy and professional practice.

ABOUT THE AUTHOR

LEGISLATIVE INVOLVEMENT

George Rosselot began working with licensure for Marriage and Family Therapists in 1974 as Legislative Chair for the Florida Association for Marriage and Family Therapy (FAMFT) and Florida Mental Health Counselors. He played a primary role in drafting the first law (1983) and revised the law effective in 1988. He was President of FAMFT, served on the American Association for Marriage and Family Therapy Committee (AAMFT) for Legislative Grants, and was honored as a Fellow by AAMFT for his legislative accomplishments establishing Marriage and Family Therapy as a profession by State Law. He received recognition for outstanding leadership at the AAMFT National Convention in 1986, was issued the first Marriage and Family Therapy license by the Florida Department of Professional Regulation (DPR) honoring his accomplishments with regard to the first licensing of Marriage and Family Therapists in the State, served as consultant to DPR for rule making and examination development for Florida Marriage and Family

APPENDIX III

Therapists, and was elected Chair of Division II Presidents Council. He has been called on as a consultant by AAMFT administrators and various division leaders.

In 1973, he founded a private interdisciplinary group practice in Tallahassee, Florida. As a clinician in full time private practice, he has dealt with the complex issues where law, regulation, and intraprofessional systems mesh at a grass roots level. He was one of the pioneers to activate and design a Coalition of Interdisciplinary Professionals within the State of Florida. He has extensive understanding and experience in the political arena involving legislative and intraprofessional issues.

In 1992 he was a key leader encouraging lawmakers to place Marriage and Family Therapists, Clinical Social Workers and Mental Health Counselors in the Judicial Evidence Code defining each as a Psychotherapist with confidentiality as stated in the State Evidence Code. He also assisted with the professional law change providing that 490 and 491 Chapters be a "Practice Act" defining each

ABOUT THE AUTHOR

profession therein, thus increasing the Florida Standards of Psychologists, School Psychologists, Clinical Social Workers, Marriage and Family Therapists, and Mental Health Counselors who formerly held only title protection.

Mr. Rosselot holds firm to his primary philosophy that the "Best Interest of the Public" must always be first and foremost regarding professionalism, services provided, ethics, and especially law and regulatory rules.

www.ingramcontent.com/pod-product-compliance
Lightning Source LLC
Chambersburg PA
CBHW031258290426
44109CB00012B/644